FRENCH FOOD FOR EVERYONE

le dîner

(dinner)

MARDI MICHELS

author of
In the French kitchen with kids

For Neil. I can't think of anyone I'd rather share dinner with.

MARDI MICHELS is a full-time French teacher to elementary school-aged boys and the author of www.eatlivetravelwrite.com - a blog focusing on culinary adventures near and far. As part of her job, she runs cooking classes for boys aged 7 to 14. Mardi grew up in Australia, lived and taught in Paris for over five years and now calls Toronto home. In 2014, Mardi and her husband purchased a home in southwest France, which they operate as a vacation rental property (www.neracvacationrental.com). Mardi also offers French cooking and baking classes for adults and children around Toronto (www.eatlivetravelwrite.com/classes). Her first book, *In the French kitchen with kids*, was published July 31st 2018 (Appetite by Random House). Her second book, *French Food for Everyone*, will be published chapter by chapter starting with *le goûter (after-school snacks)* in September 2021 and *le dîner* (dinner) in December 2021. Read more at: www.eatlivetravelwrite.com/books

Library and Archives of Canada Cataloguing in Publication is available upon request.

ISBN: 978-1-7778365-2-8
ebook ISBN: 978-1-7778365-3-5

Author photo by Steve Polak
Photography by Mardi Michels
Illustrations by Lisa Nunamaker
Design by LeAnna Weller Smith, Weller Smith Design

Published in Canada by MLM Publications.

www.eatlivetravelwrite.com

Pub Date: December 2021
First Printing

"French Food for Everyone" is a follow up to the best-selling "In the French kitchen with kids" and was inspired by the students in my online cooking classes in 2020 and 2021, when Covid restrictions forced us to pivot things like cooking classes to online platforms. Although I've known all along that French food is really much simpler to make than many people believe (so easy even kids can make "fancy" French dishes!), over the course of a year's worth of online classes, I was even more encouraged by the great success my students were having with my recipes. After a few months, one of my students remarked on the "recipe book" they had created from the online class recipes and I realised that I had enough recipes for another cookbook. However, instead of going the traditional publishing route this time, I am releasing the book one chapter at a time so you can get cooking and baking sooner! I hope you love this new, more accessible format!

Introduction

The words "*à table*" translate literally as "to the table" but are used to let everyone know that a meal is ready. These days, dinner might be the only meal that families enjoy together, around an actual table, *un moment de convivialité*, as the French might say, where stories about the day are shared over a meal.

Often, when people hear "French food" they assume the recipe will be too complicated, the ingredients too hard to find, the techniques too fussy for them to attempt at home. In my first book, *In the French kitchen with kids*, I proved otherwise. Children and adults alike all over the world discovered that French food was easy to make at home. That good quality ingredients can be transformed with simple techniques to make delicious dishes.

Ok, but what about *le dîner* – the main meal of the day – isn't that going to require some more complex skills? Not necessarily, even though some of them have reputations for being hard to make – (French) Onion Soup (p 12), I'm looking at you! But when you look at the recipes themselves, there's nothing too complicated for a home cook.

Some of the recipes (i.e. the aforementioned soup) do take time - the *Daube de Boeuf* (p 29) is one you'll want to plan for (it's an "all afternoon to cook" meal but with very little hands-on time) but many of them are simple enough to make even on a weeknight.

These dozen recipes are by no means representative of the breadth of French cuisine; rather these are dishes I've come to love over the years living in and travelling to France. Nostalgic dishes (*Bavette à l'échalote*, p 33, comfort food dishes (*Tartiflette*, p 18) and Bistro favourites (*Daube de Boeuf*, p 29) meet beloved classics like *Poulet rôti* (p 26, Roast Chicken but with a quick twist). I hope you will enjoy bringing a little bit of France to your table through this collection of recipes and maybe learn a little kitchen French or French history along the way?

—Mardi

INGREDIENTS

I think the most important note to make about the ingredients in these recipes is about the vegetables. I've included both weight (in grams and oz), and an estimate of how many of a certain vegetable this might be. Why? Well, because my "medium onion" might not look or weigh the same as your "medium onion" and when you dice it, your pieces might be smaller or larger than mine, meaning your "1 cup of diced onions" might contain way more or less than mine. Weight is helpful because it ensures that the balance of ingredients in the recipe is right. This is especially important in recipes like the *Papillote de poisson à la ratatouille* (p 37) where "whole" vegetables won't be used, just portions of them. It's all about the ratios! Where it makes sense, I've included volume measurements of vegetables.

You'll see in the Equipment suggestions that I *strongly* recommend a kitchen scale – they're not just for bakers! If you don't have one or don't have access to one, produce stores and farmers' markets will have scales and don't be shy to ask for a certain quantity of something.

For this collection of recipes, Neil Phillips of VinCetera Group (and my in-house wine expert!) has put his WSET Level 3 and French Wine Scholar certifications to good use and offered some pairing suggestions for each of the dishes. Look for this icon to pair your dish with a French wine or an alternative that might be easier to find.

EQUIPMENT

For this collection of dishes, each recipe includes a "must have" piece of equipment (typically the baking dish or pot the recipe cooks in). Here are some items you will want to have on hand.

- ⊘ kitchen scale (for the most accuracy)

- ⊘ measuring cups and spoons

- ⊘ liquid measuring jugs

- ⊘ timer (a separate one from the one on your phone - you don't know how many times I have accidentally cancelled a timer when I was fiddling with my phone!)

- ⊘ wooden spoons

- ⊘ various sized mixing and prep bowls

- ⊘ garlic press (optional but useful)

- ⊘ parchment paper

- ⊘ a sharp chef's knife

- ⊘ cutting board

- ⊘ 1 x large oven-ready pot (approx. 3-quart/2.8L capacity), like a Dutch oven

- ⊘ 1 x small skillet (approx. 8-9 inches/20-23cm in diameter)

- ⊘ 1 x large, heavy skillet (approx. 12 inches/30cm in diameter and 2 inches/ 5cm deep)

- ⊘ 1 x a large, deep preferably non-stick 3-quart (2.8 L) ovenproof skillet (approx. 10 inches/ 25 cm in diameter)

- ⊘ 1 x rectangular ovenproof baking dish (approx. 8 x 11 inches/ 20 x 28cm and 2 inches/ 5 cm deep)

- ⊘ A couple of deep baking dishes - rectangular or round

- ⊘ 1 x large rimmed sheet pan (18 x 13 inches/ 46 x 33cm)

les recettes - recipes

soupe à l oignon gratinée (« French » onion soup) 12

endives au jambon gratinées (endives with ham and mornay sauce) 15

tartiflette (cheesy potato bake) 18

hachis parmentier végétarien (vegetarian shepherd's pie) 21

poulet basquaise (Basque chicken and pepper stew) 22

blanquette de poulet (creamy chicken stew) 25

poulet rôti rapide (quick roast chicken) 26

daube de bœuf (rich beef stew) 29

steak au poivre (pepper steak with cognac cream sauce) 30

bavette à l'échalote (flank steak with red wine and shallot sauce) 33

filets de poisson "meunière" (buttery lemony fish) 34

papillote de poisson à la ratatouille
(fish « en papillote » with ratatouille) 37

soupe à l oignon gratinée

(French) Onion Soup

Is there any dish more emblematic of a French bistro than a steaming bowl of richly flavoured onion soup? There's some debate as to the origins of this dish – some say it was invented when King Louis XV returned from a hunt, starving, and could only find onions, champagne and butter in the kitchen which were subsequently transformed into a version of the dish we know today. Others suggest it was brought to King Louis XV's court by the Duke of Lorraine, (formerly the King of Poland) Stanislas Leszczynski, who tasted a version prepared by Chef Nicholas Appert and who loved it so much he insisted on getting the recipe and preparing it for the King. However it was invented, it's a testament to time transforming ordinary ingredients into something really magical.

SERVES 6-8

3 tablespoons olive oil

900g (approx. 2lb) sweet onions such as Vidalia, halved and thinly sliced (approx. 7 cups when trimmed and sliced)

3 tablespoons (45g/ 1.6oz) salted butter

1 teaspoon fresh thyme leaves

1 tablespoon granulated sugar

1/2 cup (120ml) dry white wine

6 cups (1 1/2 litres) beef broth

Flaky sea salt and freshly-ground black pepper, to taste

TO SERVE:

Toasted baguette

Grated Gruyère or Swiss cheese (a generous handful per bowl of soup)

YOU WILL NEED:

1 deep, Dutch oven-type pot (approx. 2-quart/ 2L capacity)

Oven-proof soup bowls

In France, this is simply known as Soupe à l'Oignon Gratinée, there's no "French" in the name!

A Northern Rhone or Languedoc Viognier. Failing that, a Fino Sherry.

METHOD

1. Heat the oil in a large, heavy pot over medium-high heat.

2. Add the onions and stir to coat well with the oil.

3. Lower the heat to medium-low and cook the onions for 10 minutes, stirring from time to time so they don't stick. The onions will be starting to colour at this point.

4. Add the butter and thyme to the skillet and stir to coat the onions well with the butter. Reduce the heat to medium-low.

5. Cook the onions for 10 minutes over medium-low heat, stirring occasionally and keeping an eye on the pan. If they look like they are starting to stick, lower the heat slightly. At this stage, the onions will be golden.

6. Add the sugar and stir to coat the onions.

7. Cook the onions for 15 more minutes over medium-low heat, stirring fairly constantly during this time. Now the onions will really be starting to colour, turning a rich golden brown the more you cook them.

8. Increase the heat to medium-high and add the wine to the pan, scraping any browned bits off the bottom of the pan. When the wine has evaporated, slowly pour in the broth and stir.

9. Increase the heat and bring the stock to a boil, then cover the pot and lower the heat, simmering for 10 minutes.

10. Set aside to cool slightly before assembling the dish. Season to taste with salt and pepper.

ASSEMBLE AND SERVE:

1. Pre-heat your oven grill/ broiler to high.

2. Place soup bowls on a baking tray lined with a silicone baking mat (so the bowls don't slip).

3. Ladle soup into each bowl, filling them around 3/4 full.

4. Place 1-2 slices of toasted baguette on the top of each bowl of soup and top with a generous helping of the grated cheese.

5. Place the tray under the grill and cook until the cheese is golden brown and melted.

6. Allow to cool ever so slightly before you serve (with a warning that the cheese is hot!).

This may seem like a LONG time to cook the onions but it's the only way to get the flavour (and colour). Don't plan on multitasking in the kitchen when you make this. Stay close to the stove and keep an eye on the onions!

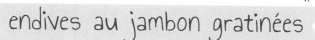

endives au jambon gratinées

(Endives with Ham and Mornay Sauce)

I was first introduced to this dish by my Belgian host mother, Francine, when I spent a year in Brussels as a 17-year-old exchange student. Growing up in Australia I'd never heard of an endive, let alone tasted one. I always sat in the kitchen chatting with Francine as she cooked (I learned a lot of French this way!) and still remember when she was describing this dish to me – a bitter leaved vegetable, slightly caramelised, wrapped in ham and smothered in a *Mornay* sauce (*Béchamel* with added cheese). Ok then. Sounded...interesting. It's actually wildly delicious and the flavours play well together! Perfect served as a side or with a green salad and plenty of crusty baguette for a main course.

PREPARE THE ENDIVES:

1. Preheat the oven to 375°F/ 190°C.

2. Remove any loose outer leaves from the endives, keeping the base intact.

3. Melt the butter in a shallow sauté or frying pan (large enough to fit all the endives in at once, if possible) over medium heat and add the endives.

4. Sauté endives over medium heat for approximately 8 minutes, until they start to brown, turning them to coat them in the butter from time to time.

5. Sprinkle the sugar over the endives and continue to cook until the endives start to caramelize approximately 2-3 minutes (they will be golden brown in parts).

6. Remove the pan from the heat and set aside so the endives cool slightly (you can remove the endives from the pan if you like to cool them faster).

MAKE THE MORNAY SAUCE:

1. Heat the milk until it's just about boiling (bubbles should form around the edge of the pot) in medium pot on the stovetop or in a microwave.

2. Heat the butter over medium heat in medium-sized pot.

3. Stir in the flour and cook for 2 minutes, stirring constantly until it smells nutty.

4. Whisk in the warm milk and continue to cook, whisking constantly until the mixture starts to thicken slightly (about 2 minutes). It will be the texture of drinking yoghurt.

5. Remove from the heat and add 1/2 cup grated cheese and continue to whisk until cheese is melted into the mixture. Season to taste with salt and pepper. Set aside.

ASSEMBLE AND BAKE:

1. Wrap the cooled, caramelized endives in a slice of ham and place seam-side down in the prepared baking dish. Pour over the Mornay sauce, covering the endives completely.

2. Bake at 400°F/ 200°C for 25 minutes.

3. Heat the broiler/grill to high. Sprinkle the remaining 1/4 cup of grated cheese over the top of the baking dish and broil until golden brown and bubbling (5-7 minutes - start to check on it at 5 minutes).

SERVES 2 AS A MAIN COURSE,
6 AS A SIDE DISH

FOR THE ENDIVES:

6 small endives (approximately 80g/ 2.8oz each – if your endives are larger, cut them in halves lengthways, you might only need 3-4)

2 tablespoons unsalted butter

2 tablespoons granulated sugar

FOR THE MORNAY SAUCE:

2 tablespoons butter

2 tablespoons all-purpose flour

3/4 cup (180ml) milk

1/2 cup (50g/ 1.8oz) grated cheese like Gruyère or Emmenthal

Flaky sea salt and freshly-ground black pepper, to taste

TO ASSEMBLE:

6 slices of ham (large enough to wrap the endives in)

1/4 cup (30g/ 1oz) grated cheese like Gruyère or Emmenthal

YOU WILL NEED:

1 ovenproof baking dish that your endives fit snugly into.

A white Cotes du Rhone or Jura. For red, try a Beaujolais. Alternatively, a Californian Fumé Blanc.

1. Before you start.

   Make sure you have a baking dish where the endives fit snugly. If the dish is too large, the endives will swim in the sauce and the sauce may split. If you have larger endives (weigh them!) you might like to cut them in halves, in which case you'll need less.

2. Caramelize the endives.

   Melt the butter in a shallow sauté or frying pan (large enough to fit all the endives in at once, if possible) over medium heat and sauté until they start to brown, turning them from time to time. Next, sprinkle the sugar over the endives and continue to cook until theystart to caramelize. Remove the pan from the heat and set aside so the endives cool slightly.

3. Prepare the endives.

Wrap the caramelized endives in a slice of ham and place seam-side down in the prepared baking dish. They should be snug in the dish.

4. Assemble the dish.

Pour over the *Mornay* sauce, covering the endives completely. The sauce might not "pour" very well so just do your best to smooth it over the endives evenly.

tartiflette

(Cheesy Potato Bake)

Tartiflette is a dish from the Savoie region in the French Alps, popular there because it's the perfect way to warm up after a day's skiing. It might not sound like much - potatoes/ onions/ bacon/ cheese, but the ingredients work together in a magical way creating a dish that feels like a warm hug on a cold day. Traditionally made with Reblochon cheese (see below for substitutions), this can be served as a side dish or with a side salad as a hearty main course with steamed or sautéed vegetables.

SERVES 2 AS A MAIN, 4 AS A SIDE

3/4 lb (340g) potatoes, peeled (this is about 1 large or 2 small potatoes)

1 tablespoon olive oil

4 slices bacon (approx. 100g/ 3.5oz), roughly chopped in small cubes or strips (about 3/4 cup, chopped)

1 medium onion (approx. 150g/ 5.3oz), finely diced (about 1 cup diced)

2 large cloves garlic, minced

Flaky sea salt and freshly-ground black pepper

1/4 cup (60ml) dry white wine

1/4 cup (60ml) heavy cream (35%)

250g/ 9oz Reblochon cheese sliced into 0.2 inch/ 1/2cm strips

fresh thyme, to garnish

YOU WILL NEED:

1 ovenproof baking dish, large enough to hold the sliced potatoes, bacon/onion mixture and cheese. I used a round (9 inch/ 23cm) baking dish

METHOD

1. Pre-heat oven to 400°F/ 200°C.

2. Place the potatoes in a large pot and fill it with cold water to just cover the potatoes.

3. Bring the water to a boil and cook until the potatoes are tender enough to insert a sharp knife in the middle. They should not be completely cooked at this point. This will take around 10 minutes. Drain and allow to cool slightly.

4. Heat the oil over medium heat in a medium skillet. Add the bacon to the skillet and fry for a couple of minutes.

5. Add the onions and garlic to the skillet and cook, stirring occasionally until the onions are translucent (3-5 minutes). Season with salt and pepper.

6. Pour in the wine. Use a wooden spoon to scrape the bottom of the pan clean. Continue to cook until the wine has evaporated. Set the pan aside to cool.

7. Slice the cooled potatoes into thin (0.2 inch/ 1/2cm) slices.

8. In an ovenproof dish large enough to hold all the ingredients, layer half the onions, garlic and bacon.

9. Top with half the potato slices.

10. Repeat the process, layering the rest of the onions, then bacon, then the remaining potatoes.

11. Pour over the cream, shaking the pan slightly to distribute it evenly through the ingredients.

12. Top with the strips of cheese – note that it will not cover the top of the dish entirely - you will have some gaps and that's ok.

13. Bake for 25-30 minutes at 400°F/ 200°C until the cheese is bubbling and golden.

14. Remove from the oven and allow to cool slightly before serving. Garnish with fresh thyme.

Alsatian Pinot Gris. Alternatively, a South African Chenin Blanc.

If you can't find Reblochon, Oka, Epoisses, Kenogami or any soft washed rind cheese will work.

hachis parmentier végétarien
(Vegetarian Shepherd's Pie)

Hachis Parmentier is a classic French comfort food dish. Typically made from leftover cooked meat that's chopped into small pieces (hachis means food that is finely diced or minced) in a gravy-like sauce, topped with mashed potatoes. The meat filling can include vegetables (peas, carrots, turnips) but it's definitely a meat-heavy dish. This vegetarian version with celery, carrots, mushrooms and lentils is lighter but no less comforting. Even my biggest carnivore taste testers ask for this again and again!

MAKE THE FILLING:

1. Heat the oil over medium-high heat in a large, heavy skillet.

2. Add the onion and garlic and cook for apbout 3 minutes (until the onions are just starting to soften but not colour).

3. Add the celery, carrots and mushrooms and stir to combine. Cook for about 5 minutes or until the mushrooms are just starting to release their juices.

4. Add the lentils and stock, stir well and bring to the boil.

5. Add the peas, stir to combine and cook for 2 minutes.

6. Remove the pan from the heat and set aside. Season to taste with salt and pepper.

7. Pre-heat the oven to 400°F/ 200°F.

MAKE THE MASHED POTATO TOPPING:

1. Place the potatoes in a large pot of cold water and place on high heat. Bring to the boil and cook until the potatoes are "fork tender" (you should be able to easily mash them with a fork).

2. Drain the potatoes and place them back into the pot, off the heat.

3. Mash the potatoes until smooth. Do not place the pot on the heat again.

4. Add the cream, butter and salt and use a wooden spoon or a rubber spatula to combine all ingredients, until smooth and creamy.

ASSEMBLE THE DISH:

1. Check your oven is at 400°F/ 200°F. Place the filling in a deep, oven-ready casserole dish, spreading it evenly over the bottom of the dish.

2. Spoon the potatoes on top of the filling. I place a scoop in each corner and one in the middle then use a rubber spatula to smooth the potatoes to the edges.

3. Bake for 15-20 minutes or until the potatoes are crispy and golden and the filling is bubbling away (you might see some of the filling peeking out under the potatoes). Depending on your oven, this time may vary. Keep an eye on the dish and check on it after 10 minutes.

SERVES 4-6

FOR THE FILLING:

2 tablespoons olive oil

1 medium onion (approx. 150g/ 5.3oz) finely diced (about 1 cup)

2 cloves garlic, minced

1 teaspoon dried *Herbes de Provence* (or thyme)

2 celery stalks (approx. 200g/ 7oz total), peeled and finely diced

2 small carrots (approx. 200g/ 7oz total), finely diced

2 cups (approx. 250g/ 8oz) finely diced white mushrooms

1 cup (from 1 x 540ml can) cooked green lentils, drained and rinsed

1 cup (240ml) vegetable stock

Flaky sea salt and freshly-ground black pepper

1/2 cup frozen peas

FOR THE POTATO TOPPING:

2lbs (approx. 900g) white potatoes peeled and chopped into 1 inch/2cm cubes

1/4 cup (60mls) heavy cream (35%)

2 tablespoons unsalted butter

1/2 teaspoon fine sea salt

freshly ground pepper

YOU WILL NEED:

1 rectangular ovenproof baking dish (mine is 8 x 11 inches/ 20 x 28cm and 2 inches/ 5 cm deep)

Chopping the mushrooms finely takes a little bit of time. If you want to save time, use a food processor but do it in batches otherwise they will be too finely chopped on the bottom of the bowl and not finely chopped enough on top.

Red Bourgogne or Passetoutgrains. Alternatively, Italian Barbera.

poulet basquaise

(Basque Chicken and Pepper Stew)

Travelling through the Basque Country in Southwest France or northern Spain, you might notice a lot of red and green everywhere from street signs to cookware, table linen and dishes. Those are the colours of the Basque flag (with white) and this recipe is a nod to that (white chicken with red and green peppers). This colorful dish is seasoned with the local-to-the-region *Piment d'Espelette* (Espelette chili powder), a spice you'll see all over. Brought to the area from Mexico in the 16th Century, it's used in many dishes in the region. It's not super spicy, the heat is subtle. If you travel in the Basque Country, you'll see the peppers drying in the sun everywhere! Serve with steamed white rice.

INGREDIENTS (SERVES 4)

8 chicken thighs (bone in, skin on)

4 tablespoons olive oil, divided

1/2 cup (120 ml) warm chicken stock

1 medium onion (approx. 150g/ 5.3oz), halved and thinly sliced

4 cloves garlic, minced

2 red peppers (approx. 400g/ 14oz total), cored, seeded and sliced into 1/2 inch/ 1cm strips

2 green peppers (approx. 400g/ 14oz) total, cored, seeded and sliced into 1/2 inch/ 1cm strips

1 teaspoon dried thyme or *Herbes de Provence*

1 teaspoon flaky sea salt

1/2 teaspoon freshly ground black pepper

1 teaspoon *Piment d'Espelette* (or you can use 1/2 teaspoon chili powder)

3 cups diced tomatoes and their juices (one 796ml/ 28oz can)

YOU WILL NEED:

1 large, deep preferably non-stick 3-quart (2.8 L) ovenproof skillet (approx. 10 inches/ 25 cm in diameter)

1. Pre-heat oven to 375°F/ 190°F.

2. Heat 2 tablespoons of the olive oil in a large, deep preferably non-stick 3-quart (2.8 L) ovenproof skillet (approx. 10 inches/ 25 cm in diameter), over medium-high heat.

3. Place the thighs skin-side down and cook until nicely browned (6-8 minutes). Flip the chicken and cook for a further 5 minutes. Set aside on a plate. (You might need to do this in batches – 4 thighs at a time - so that the pan isn't crowded).

4. Keep the skillet on the medium-high heat and add a splash of the chicken stock to the pan. Use a wooden spatula to scrape up any browned bits. Do not throw these out, they will add a lot of flavour to your dish.

5. Once the liquid has evaporated, heat the remaining 2 tablespoons olive oil in the skillet.

6. Add the onions and the garlic and cook, stirring occasionally, until soft but not browned (around 5 minutes). If the onions start to stick, add a splash of the chicken stock and scrape the bottom of the pan as needed.

7. Add the peppers, thyme, salt, pepper and *Piment d'Espelette* (or chili powder). Stir to combine all ingredients well, then cover and cook on medium heat for 5 minutes. Keep an eye on the vegetables and add a splash of chicken stock if the pan starts to look dry.

8. Add the tomatoes and rest of the stock (you shouldn't have much left at all), stir well and bring to a boil.

9. Add the chicken back into the pan, skin side up, placing it between the peppers evenly around the skillet. Spoon a little of the juices on top of the chicken pieces.

10. Cook, uncovered for 40 minutes at 375°F/ 190°F.

11. Remove from the oven, stir well and allow to sit for about 5 minutes or until the sauce stops bubbling. If there is too much liquid for your liking, you can reduce the sauce over medium heat on the stovetop for a few minutes.

White dry Jurançon; Irouléguy red or Right Bank Bordeaux. Alternatively, Chilean Merlot.

blanquette de poulet
(Creamy Chicken Stew)

Blanquette is the sort of thing you might find on a *prix fixe* menu at a French bistro, an unassuming sort of dish but one that you should know how to make! *Blanquette* refers to a light meat (typically veal) stewed in a white sauce, traditionally thickened with a roux (flour and butter) and egg yolks. This version is slightly simplified in that it doesn't involve making a roux but it's no less flavourful. It's a simple comforting meal that comes together quickly, even on a weeknight. Serve with steamed white rice and sprinkle with fresh herbs.

1. In a large, deep heavy skillet, heat the oil and butter over medium-high heat.

2. Add the chicken and cook, stirring from time to time, until it's just starting to brown on the outside (it will not be fully cooked on the inside), approx. 5-6 minutes (depending on the size of your chicken pieces).

3. Remove the chicken from the pan and drain on a plate covered in a paper towel.

4. Add the carrot, celery and onion to the pan with the fresh thyme, a big pinch of salt and a few grounds of black pepper. Cook over medium heat until the vegetables are just starting to soften (3-4 minutes).

5. Add the mushrooms and cook until the mushrooms are starting to brown and release their juices (3-4 minutes).

6. Add the flour and mix until all the vegetables are completely coated.

7. Add 1 cup of the stock and cook until the liquid is starting to thicken into a sauce.

8. Add the chicken back into the pot, then the rest of the stock and increase the heat to high. Bring the mixture to a boil.

9. Once the mixture is bubbling, reduce the heat to medium-low and simmer for approximately 10 minutes, or until the liquid has reduced to a thick "sauce". It should look like a slightly watery stew at this point.

10. Reduce the heat to low and add the cream. Stir through and cook over low heat until desired sauce consistency is reached.

11. Season to taste with salt and pepper and sprinkle with fresh herbs to serve.

SERVES 6

1 tablespoon olive oil

1 tablespoon unsalted butter

1 1/2 lb (675g) skinless, boneless chicken breasts, cut into bite-sized cubes

2 medium carrots (300g/ 10.5oz total), peeled and finely diced (approx. 2 cups)

2 small celery stalks (150g/ 5.3oz total), finely diced (1 1/4 cups)

1 medium onion (150g/ 5.3oz total), finely diced (1 1/4 cups)

2 teaspoons fresh thyme leaves

Approx. 3 cups (227g/ 7oz) thinly sliced white or cremini mushrooms

1/4 cup (38g/ 1.3oz) all-purpose flour

2 cups (500ml) chicken stock

1/4 cup (60ml) heavy cream (35%)

Flaky sea salt and freshly-ground black pepper

TO SERVE:

fresh thyme or parsley

YOU WILL NEED:

1 large, heavy skillet (approx. 12 inches/ 30cm in diameter and 2 inches/ 5cm deep)

White Bourgogne. Alternatively, dry German Riesling.

poulet rôti rapide
(Quick Roast Chicken)

At the Saturday morning market in Nérac (our "local" when we are at *maison de la fontaine*), there's a roast chicken stand, just as there is at most French food markets. The smell of the rotisserie is intoxicating, it's hard to resist. And nearly as good as the roasted birds? The roasted potatoes that are cooked in the chicken fat. It's the ultimate "fast food" and something we treat ourselves to at least once a trip! At home, we love a good roast chicken (see: "Mr Neil's Roast Chicken" from *In the French kitchen with kids*) but sometimes I don't feel like "dealing" with a whole chicken (and I know from some of my recipe testers that they don't either). Solution? Flavourful chicken thighs. A roast chicken is a one pan recipe anyway, why not make it even easier by using thighs? The finished dish is a showstopper to serve family-style. A green salad or steamed green beans would be a nice accompaniment to this dish.

SERVES 4-6, DEPENDING ON APPETITES

3 tablespoons olive oil (plus up to 4 more tablespoons for coating the chicken)

2 teaspoons dried *Herbes de Provence* (or thyme)

1 teaspoon *Piment d'Espelette* (or smoked paprika)

1 teaspoon flaky sea salt

a few generous grounds of freshly ground black pepper

1 lb (454g) new or fingerling potatoes, cut into slices approx. 1 inch/ 2cm wide

2 medium carrots (approx. 300g/ 10.6oz total), cut into 1 inch/ 2cm cubes or half moons

2 medium onions (approx. 300g/ 10.6oz total), cut into thick (about 1 inch/ 2cm) slices (too thin and they will burn)

6 cloves garlic, peeled and roughly chopped

8 bone-in, skin-on chicken thighs

YOU WILL NEED:

1 large, rimmed sheet pan (18 x 13 inches/ 46 x 33cm)

Chinon or Bourgueil from the Loire. Alternatively, Etna Rosso or Bianco from Sicily.

1. Pre-heat the oven to 450°F/ 230°C.

2. On a large sheet pan, combine the oil, Herbes de Provence, *Piment d'Espelette*, salt, pepper, potatoes, carrots, onions and garlic and mix with your hands (it's messy but easiest!) until the vegetables are well-coated with the oil and spices.

3. Rub the chicken thighs, skin side down into the oil mixture on the bottom of the pan, creating a space for each piece as you do. Once the chicken is coated with a bit of the oil, place the chicken thighs, skin side up around the sheet pan. Make sure the chicken is not sitting on top of any of the vegetables otherwise those ones will not crisp up!

4. If you need a little more oil on the chicken, use a pastry brush to brush about 1/2 teaspoon oil onto each thigh.

5. Roast the chicken and vegetables for about 45 minutes. The vegetables should be crispy and fully cooked and the chicken should register an internal temperature of 165°F.

6. If at this point, your chicken is cooked through and your vegetables are nice and crispy, but the skin of your chicken isn't quite brown/ crispy enough for you,

7. Remove the chicken thighs from the vegetables and place them on a clean tray. Broil for 3-5 minutes until they are brown/ crispy enough. Place them back with the vegetables and serve, family-style. A green salad or steamed green beans would be a nice accompaniment to this dish.

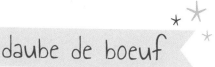
daube de boeuf

(Rich Beef Stew)

I feel like every French family probably has a *daube de boeuf* recipe in their repertoire, probably handed down from generation to generation. The word *daube* (thought to come from the Spanish *dobar*, meaning "to braise") refers to not only the dish but also the method of braising meats and vegetables with herbs in red wine and stock. A staple on many bistro menus, this is essentially a hearty beef stew that cooks low and slow and makes your kitchen smell amazing! Serve with buttered egg noodles or plenty of fresh baguette to sop up all those juices. A green salad or a side of steamed green beans is a nice addition too.

1. Pre-heat the oven to 300°F/ 150°C.

2. Mix the flour with the salt and pepper and place in a large, shallow dish.

3. A few at a time, roll the cubes of beef in the flour mixture, shaking to remove excess flour. Place on a large plate and continue until all the beef cubes are coated. Discard the flour mix.

4. Heat 1 tablespoon of the oil in a large oven-ready pot (around a 3-quart/2.8L capacity) over medium-high heat. Brown the beef in batches (so as not to crowd the pan). Remove the browned beef from the pan, place on a plate and cover with tinfoil. Continue until all beef is browned. You may need to add up to 2 more tablespoons of oil as you work through the beef.

5. Reduce the heat to medium and add the wine. Use a wooden spoon or spatula to scrape any brown bits left on the bottom of the pan. The liquid should evaporate completely before you continue. If it does not and you have a floury paste, scrape it out onto the browned beef – you'll add this back into the stew for extra flavour.

6. Add 1 tablespoon of oil and then the garlic and onions and gently cook for 3-4 minutes.

7. Add the carrots and stir to coat well with the garlic and onion mixture.

8. Pour the stock into the pan, increase the heat and bring to the boil.

9. Add the tomato paste and *Bouquet Garni* and stir to combine. Season to taste with salt and pepper.

10. Place the beef back in the pot and remove from the heat. Place the pot in the oven and cook for 2 1/2 – 3 hours, uncovered, stirring from time to time, until the beef is tender.

11. Remove the pot from the oven, remove the *Bouquet Garni* and allow the stew to sit for a few minutes. As it sits the sauce will thicken slightly. If you want to reduce the sauce more, you can heat gently over medium heat on the stovetop until it reduces to your liking.

SERVES 4-6

1 1/2 lbs (approx. 675g) stewing beef (NOT lean) cut into 3/4 inch/ 2cm cubes.

1 cup all-purpose flour

1 teaspoon fine sea salt

1 teaspoon freshly ground black pepper

2-4 tablespoons olive oil

1/2 cup (120ml) fruity red wine

1 large onion (approx. 250g/ 9oz), diced

4 cloves garlic, roughly chopped

2 large carrots (approx. 400g/ 14 oz total), cut into thick half moons

1 1/2 cups (375ml) beef stock

1/4 cup (60ml) tomato paste

1 *Bouquet Garni* (see note)

Flaky sea salt and freshly-ground black pepper

Fresh parsley, to garnish

YOU WILL NEED:

1 large oven-ready pot (approx. 3-quart/ 2.8L capacity)

For a Bouquet Garni, place a small handful of fresh parsley, fresh thyme, fresh rosemary, a strip of orange peel and 2 large bay leaves in a piece of cheesecloth and tie it closed with kitchen twine. If you don't have cheesecloth, you can simply tie all this together with kitchen twine but you might lose some in the cooking process.

Ideally, the red wine you used to cook with. Southern Rhone red such as Gigondas, Vacqueyras or Lirac. Alternatively, Austrian Zweigelt or Spanish Rioja.

steak au poivre

(Pepper Steak with Cognac Cream Sauce)

This is a classic bistro dish that feels fancy but which doesn't take any time at all to prepare. The most important thing here is to make sure your steak is cooked correctly and the best piece of equipment you can invest in is an instant-read thermometer. This way you can cook the steaks to everyone's liking! Serve this with roasted potatoes, fries or mashed potatoes and something green like a salad or steamed green beans (with a pat of butter and a sprinkle of salt, *bien sûr!*).

SERVES 2

FOR THE STEAK:

2 x filet mignon steaks (approx. 170g/ 6oz each)

About 1/4 cup coarsely-ground black pepper

TO COOK THE STEAK:

1 tablespoon olive oil

1 tablespoon (15g/ 0.5oz) salted butter

2 cloves garlic, smashed but not peeled

a few sprigs of fresh thyme

FOR THE SAUCE:

1/2 tablespoon (8g/ 0.3oz) salted butter

1 small shallot (approx. 40g/ 1.4oz), finely diced (about 1/4 cup)

1/4 cup (60ml) Cognac or brandy

1/4 cup (60ml) heavy cream (35%)

1/4 cup (60ml) beef stock

YOU WILL NEED:

1 small skillet (approx. 8-9 inches/ 20-23cm in diameter)

An instant-read meat thermometer

PREPARE THE STEAKS:

1. Sprinkle the crushed peppercorns into a plate and press both sides of each steak into them, coating each side well.

2. Set the steaks aside at room temperature on a clean plate for about 20 minutes.

COOK THE STEAKS:

1. Melt the butter and olive oil in a small skillet over medium-high heat. When the butter is melted and bubbling, add the smashed garlic and thyme and swirl the pan to coat the garlic and thyme with the melted butter.

2. Push the garlic and thyme to the side of the skillet and place the steaks in the pan (it should sizzle as you add the meat, if not, wait a few more seconds).

3. Cook the steaks for about 3 minutes on each side, until the pepper crust is crunchy and the internal temperature of the steak is 63°C (145°F) for medium-rare, 71°C (160°F) for medium and 77°C (170°F) for well-done. Remove the smashed garlic and thyme from the pan.

4. Place the cooked steaks on a clean plate and tent with tinfoil until you are ready to serve.

MAKE THE SAUCE:

1. In the same skillet you cooked the steaks in, add the butter and melt over medium-high heat.

2. Add the shallot and cook for 2-3 minutes until softened.

3. Add the Cognac and scrape the bottom of the pan as the alcohol cooks off. You want to cook this until the liquid has mostly reduced.

4. Reduce the heat to low and stir in the cream until it's just combined.

5. Stir in the beef stock and add back in any juices in the bottom of the plate the steaks are resting on. Cook until the sauce is slightly thickened (it's not very thick at all) and is shiny and smooth.

6. You can add the steaks back into the pan to serve or plate the steaks and spoon the sauce over.

Northern Rhone Syrah. Alternatively, an Australian Syrah from McLaren Vale.

bavette à l'échalote

(Flank Steak with Red Wine and Shallot Sauce)

When I was living in Paris as a student/ language teacher on a limited budget, I never bought or cooked red meat for myself but when I ate at a restaurant (not often!), it's what I always ordered. There was a small bistro in the Montorgueil neighbourhood where I lived that served an excellent version of this dish – melt-in-your-mouth *bavette* steak, shoestring *frites* and some green beans (for balance!) and it's where I always took visiting friends and later, where I would choose to go when I was visiting the city myself. It's probably my "go-to" dish (along with *crème brûlée*) and these days, I will order it at least once per visit! For a taste of France for dinner, serve this with *frites*. Note that I'm suggesting you cook the steak on a barbecue grill but if you don't have one, this will work well on the stovetop cooked in a little butter/ olive oil.

PREPARE THE STEAK:

1. Season both sides of the steak with salt and pepper.

2. Set the steak aside at room temperature on a clean plate for about 20 minutes.

3. About 10 minutes before you are ready to cook the steak, pre-heat the grill to high

COOK THE STEAKS:

1. Cook the steak on a grill until the internal temperature of the steak is 63°C (145°F) for medium-rare, 71°C (160°F) for medium and 77°C (170°F) for well-done.

2. Place the cooked steak on a clean plate and tent with tinfoil until you are ready to serve.

MAKE THE SAUCE:

1. In a small skillet, melt the butter and olive oil over medium-high heat until the butter is bubbling.

2. Add the shallots and cook for about 5 minutes, until the shallots are soft and just starting to brown.

3. Add the wine and scrape any brown bits off the bottom of the pan, increasing the heat to high. Cook until all but about 1 tablespoon of the liquid has evaporated.

4. Add the broth and the balsamic vinegar and cook, stirring occasionally until the sauce has reduced slightly (around 4 minutes).

5. Remove from the heat and add the butter, stirring until it is melted and the sauce is glossy.

6. Season to taste with salt and pepper.

SERVE:

1. Once the steak has rested for about 10 minutes (while you make the sauce), slice the meat against the grain on an angle.

2. Serve the sauce either on top of the steak or in a small ramekin on the side.

SERVES 2

FOR THE STEAK:

1 large flank steak (approx. 340g/ 12oz)

Flaky sea salt and freshly ground black pepper

FOR THE SAUCE:

1 tablespoon (15g) salted butter

1 tablespoon (15ml) olive oil

4 small shallots (approx. 150g/ 5.3oz), very thinly sliced

1/3 cup (80ml) red wine

1/2 cup (120ml) beef broth

1 teaspoon (5ml) balsamic vinegar

1/2 tablespoon (8g) salted butter

Flaky sea salt and freshly ground black pepper

YOU WILL NEED:

1 small skillet (approx. 8-9 inches/ 20-23cm in diameter)

An instant-read meat thermometer

If you can't find flank steak, flatiron, hangar or skirt steak will work here as well.

A Left Bank Bordeaux - ideally the one you used to make the sauce. Alternatively, an Argentinian Malbec from Mendoza.

filets de poisson « "meunière" »

(Buttery Lemony Fish)

Regular readers of my blog will know that I'm not the « biggest » fish fan but over the years, I've started to eat it more. In France, often I'll find myself choosing fish on a *prix fixe* menu over a heavier meat dish, especially if I want to save a little room for dessert! I tend to favour very simple preparations and white fish, like this one. This is a version of one I've had many times, a simplified version of the classic *meunière* preparation. Roasted potatoes make an excellent side dish here!

SERVES 2

FOR THE FISH:

1/4 cup (38g/ 1.3oz) flour

1/2 teaspoon flaky sea salt

1 teaspoon freshly-ground black pepper

2 white fish fillets (such as cod or halibut), between 150 – 200g/ 5.3 – 7oz each (1 inch/ 2.5cm thick)

3 tablespoons (45g/ 1.6oz) unsalted butter

FOR THE "SAUCE"

1 tablespoon butter

2 tablespoons fresh lemon juice

1 tablespoon lemon zest

1/4 cup chopped fresh curly parsley

TO SERVE:

Lemon wedges

Chopped fresh curly parsley

YOU WILL NEED:

1 small (approx. 9 inch/ 23 cm) shallow skillet. If you're making 4 portions, you'll need a larger skillet if you want to cook all the fish together.

1. Whisk flour, salt and pepper in a shallow dish.

2. Dip the fish fillets in the flour mixture, one at a time, making sure to coat the fish all over, patting the flour into the fish with your fingers. Set aside on a clean plate.

3. Melt the butter in a small shallow skillet over medium-high heat.

4. When the butter is bubbling, add the fish. Cook the fish 2-3 minutes on each side, being careful not to break the fish as you flip it (a small offset spatula is useful here). When the fish is cooked, it will flake easily and it will be opaque, not translucent. 5. Remove the fish from the skillet and set aside on a plate.

6. Lower the heat to medium and add 1 tablespoon of butter.

7. Once the butter is bubbling, add the lemon juice and zest. Cook until the liquid reduces slightly and looks glossy. Add the parsley and stir to combine.

8. Add the fish back into the pan and baste with a little bit of the sauce.

9. Serve with lemon wedges and extra chopped fresh parsley.

Bourgogne Saint-Bris or white Bordeaux. Alternatively, Canadian Chardonnay.

Meunière means "millers wife" and refers to the flour that the fish is coated in before it's cooked.

papillote de poisson à la ratatouille

(Fish « en papillote » with ratatouille)

Papillote (Pap-ee-ot). *Ratatouille* (Rat-a-too-ee). Are there more fun words in the French language? (Actually if you ask my students, there are. *Pamplemousse*, for example. But, I digress...). This "two for one" recipe cooks the vegetables with the fish at the same time (*en papillote* refers to a dish that's cooked and served in parchment paper or tinfoil, not to be confused with *papillote* which means the little frilly paper used to garnish lamb chops or chicken drumsticks). I personally love white fish served with ratatouille and steamed white rice and this is so easy and appealing (so much fun to have your own little "present" served for dinner). It's a perfect way to get both dishes on the table with very little hands-on time.

1. Pre-heat oven to 400°F/ 200°F and prepare a small baking tray (large enough to hold both fillets).

2. Cut 2 squares of parchment paper about twice the size of the longest side of the fish fillets.

3. In a small bowl, mix the shallot, zucchini, pepper, tomato, garlic, basil leaves, salt, black pepper and oil. Stir to combine and taste to see if you need extra pepper or salt.

4. Place the fish in the middle of each sheet of parchment on the baking tray and top each fillet with half the ratatouille mixture.

5. Bring opposite sides of the parchment together and double fold the edges. Do the same for the other ends of parchment paper and carefully tuck both ends under the fish.

6. Bake for 20 minutes then remove the tray from the oven.

7. Carefully unfold the parchment paper – there may be some liquid pooling in the bottom of the parchment so pour this off over the sink or scrap bowl.

8. Serve with steamed white rice (either serve your rice directly into the parchment or remove the fish from the parchment and lay it on top of the rice). Sprinkle with fresh herbs.

SERVES 2

2 firm white fish fillets (e.g. cod or halibut), between 150 – 200g/ 5.3 - 7oz each (1 inch/ 2.5cm thick)

1/4 cup very finely chopped shallot (about 1 shallot, 40g/ 1.4oz)

1/4 cup very finely diced zucchini (about 1/4 zucchini, 40g/ 1.4oz)

1/4 cup very finely diced bell pepper (about 1/4 pepper, 40g/ 1.4oz)

1/4 cup very finely diced eggplant (about 1/4 baby eggplant, 40g/ 1.4oz)

1/4 cup very finely diced tomato (about 4-6 cherry tomatoes, 40g/ 1.4oz)

2 large cloves garlic, minced

6 large basil leaves, finely chopped

1/4 teaspoon flaky sea salt

A few generous grinds freshly ground black pepper

1 tablespoon olive oil

Fresh parsley, thyme and basil, finely chopped, to garnish

Note that "finely diced" here means VERY fine, otherwise the vegetables won't cook by the time the fish is cooked!

White Sancerre or Provençal rosé. Alternatively, New Zealand Sauvignon Blanc.

1. **Prepare the parchment.**
   Place the fish in the middle of each sheet of parchment on the baking tray and top each fillet with half the ratatouille mixture. Cover the fish completely with the vegetables and try to cover it evenly.

2. **Make the first folds.**
   Bring opposite sides of the parchment together over top of the fish and double fold these edges together.

3. **Secure your folds.**
   Your parchment parcels don't need to be tightly wrapped but the parchment folds do. If you can manage an extra fold, do it!.

4. Fold the ends.
Now fold the ends of the parchment paper over themselves – forming a triangle makes it easier to "seal" the parchment paper more securely.

5. Wrap it up!
Tuck the short ends of the parchment paper underneath the fish. you should now have a neat-ish parcel of fish and vegetables.

6. Once the fish is cooked.
Be careful when you open the parcels after they have cooked – and there may be some liquid pooling in the bottom of the parchment parcel. Carefully and drain this off.

ACKNOWLEDGEMENTS

This chapter of *French Food for Everyone* came together during a busy term and I couldn't have done it without the following people. Massive thanks go to:

Neil for eating all these dishes multiple times, for heading to the store every time I forgot an ingredient and for your helpful wine pairings.

Lisa Nunamaker – there is truly no project that your illustrations don't enhance! Thank you for once again bringing my ideas to life so beautifully.

Mary Catherine Anderson, my chief recipe tester. Thank you for your encouragement and friendship. Recipes tested by you are always improved thanks to your knowledge and excellent questions.

My small but mighty team of recipe testers: Jonathan B, Joelle C, Lori and Andrew C, Kate H (and friends!), Alan, Henry and Josie G. Your enthusiasm for these recipes, your suggestions and questions made these dishes so much better.

Michelle B and Orest T: Thanks for coming to our Thanksgiving "cookbook recipe tasting" dinner!

My eternal cheerleaders: Dorie Greenspan, Alison Fryer, Mairlyn Smith, Jennifer Greco, Ann Mah and Lucy Vanel. Thanks for believing in me.

The students in my online cooking classes in 2020 and 2021 who helped me see just how do-able these recipes are. A special shoutout to my Fall 2021 cooking club members who spent 45 minutes on a cold November night on a Zoom call proving that kids CAN caramelize onions and not get bored (and not burn them)!

LeAnna Weller Smith. From our first Zoom call when we both showed up in French stripey tops, it felt like this partnership was meant to be. Thank you for gently guiding my vision and making such a beautiful book. Again.